Ole Skjerbæk Madsen



# Christfulness®

## An Introduction

areopagos In the Master's Light

**Christfulness®. An Introduction**
Areopagos and In the Master's Light



**Translated** from the Danish version (© 2012) by Richard Swain


**Typeset**: Pedersen og Pedersen, Århus
**Photograph back cover**: Alex Wallin

**Printing**: Print on demand by www.lulu.com

**ISBN** 978-87-993083-3-0

# Contents

## Preface

# Christfulness – a relatively new expression

The term Christfulness was first coined by the Nordic Christian organization "In the Master's Light" (I Mesterens Lys – IML)[1] in November 2011 at an event called "The Mystical Universe" in Copenhagen. We offered to pray with people for Christfulness and received some positive responses. At a subsequent "Body, Mind and Spirit" event in February 2012, also in Copenhagen, I held a seminar about Identity and Life changing, where the participants were introduced to the term Christfulness. As part of this I led a meditation based around Christfulness. One participant exclaimed "I have always known in my head that I was loved, but now I know it in my heart." The positive reception of both Christfulness as a concept and the corresponding practices designed by IML gave us the encouragement for further development. This short book is a step on the way to widening the knowledge of Christfulness as an expression of faith.

I wish to describe a process which takes us from an experience by an individual to a vision of human redemption and the healing of our planet – in a constant interplay between the individual and the relational, the personal and the universal.

Christfulness has its origins in the experience that God is with us, and comes to life in Christ. Just as the word of God became flesh in Jesus Christ, so we in Christ are given access to the nature of God.

This book explains Christfulness as an expression of faith, a spiritual experience and an attitude to life. The book is not just a theoretical work, but also encompasses practical experience. The content has been influenced by practice, and will also give the reader an insight into my own spiritual life. You will see this most evidently through the so called "inspirations" – passages which are my own experiences of God's – as Father, Son and Holy Spirit – communication of God self to me during prayer and quietness in God's presence.
The second section of the book contains a description of how we practice Christfulness.

*Ole Skjerbæk Madsen*
*Advent 2012*

# Christfulness

## Mindfulness and Christfulness – complimentary practices

Many people have heard of Mindfulness. As yet only a few have heard of Christfulness.

Briefly, Mindfulness involves an active awareness of the present, and a non-judgemental attitude to those around you. As people learn to be truly aware of the present, they can then begin to break with old and inappropriate habits and patterns of behaviour. Thus courses in Mindfulness advertise reduction in stress levels and an increased quality of life. Any techniques which can lead to such an active awareness and non-judgemental attitude are of course to be welcomed, so why then use the term Christfulness and develop practices in Christfulness?

Mindfulness has its roots in Buddhism and comprises part of the way to enlightenment, and it cannot be wholly separated from these Buddhist roots. Many courses present Mindfulness as religiously neutral exercises, which incorporate useful techniques from the spiritual psychology of the Far East. However, this does not mean that it is no longer spiritual, and that it is no longer coloured by its origins. Mindfulness can be understood as a secularised form of an Eastern inspired spirituality. Mindfulness is one part of a wave of popularised, secularised Buddhism, which you meet in spiritual and therapeutic milieus, characterised by a post-modern and fluctuating religiosity. The emphasis on awareness of the present and a non-judgemental attitude to life can similarly be found in, for example, Eckhart Tolles' *"The Power of Now"*, and also in the understanding of the illusory nature of the senses in *"A Course in Miracles"*.

Mindfulness can, as a consequence of its Buddhist background, lead to a feeling of emptiness, which can be both positive and negative. The positive effect can be a form of emptiness where the individual is freed from the illusions which bind our existence to the past and the future, and possibly the world of the senses. However, emptiness can also feel threatening, if it seems to be leading towards a feeling of one's very being dissolving away. Finally, Mindfulness can seem like a religious harassment, when courses held at work or by an external company are presented as more or less obligatory "offers", since not all people see all forms of spirituality as free from religion.

However, please don't think of Christfulness as a criticism of Mindfulness, because Christfulness has some of the same qualities as Mindfulness, namely being actively and non-judgementally aware of the present, and breaking with old patterns of behaviour. Nonetheless Christfulness is also a concept which includes what I, as a Christian, see as missing in Mindfulness. What we have here is a complimentary practice to Mindfulness. Christfulness is based on a biblical understanding of a human as a person, i.e. that a human is not merely an isolated individual, but is also formed by relationships – to God and other people. Moreover Christfulness includes a vision for humanity together.

As a Christian I have lacked a transcendent dimension in Mindfulness which can resolve the tension between active awareness of the present and non-judgement. To live in the world without judging it often involves in Mindfulness being a dispassionate observer of the situation, allowing the pain you feel to be present and allowing thoughts to flow in and out without seeking to influence them; to see them as clouds, which disappear. This is a good exercise, which helps you to be attentive to the present. But this version of non-judgement can bring with it a disengaged and dispassionate relationship to humanity and suffering in the world, an acceptance of the status quo, a fatalistic attitude to life. In this case a non-judging approach leads to a distancing from others. And here attentive awareness, as seen through the eyes of a Christian, stops being attentively aware of other people as well as the world. It is here you can clearly see Mindfulness' roots in Buddhism, for the precise purpose of Mindfulness is to help to see through the illusory nature of suffering and existence.[2] This state can be counteracted through exercises in empathy and compassion.

For the Christian, the way Jesus behaves towards others is the motivation for a non-judgemental attitude to others. The Christian lives in a "me-you" relationship with God. For the Christian there is nothing illusory about life in the world, because the world has been created and willed into existence by God. And as a being created in the image of God, the human exists in a serving relationship to the rest of living creation. This me-you relationship to God must be reflected in how we relate to fellow human beings and the whole of creation. It is this transcendence a Christian can lack as a motivational and normalising factor in Mindfulness. In Christfulness we seek to express a relationship to our fellow humans and to all of creation, influenced by Christ and the attentive and respectful attitude he showed to the people he met.
Christfulness is not new. The reader will realise that the content has always been known – both in relation to the teaching and the spiritual practice. The form of expression is new, but thoughts underlying Christfulness are a classic Christian spirituality expressed in a context where we otherwise encounter, amongst other things, practices such as Mindfulness, and Eastern inspired forms of meditation and

courses in self-improvement, and where religion is often treated with suspicion, and described in negative sounding expressions such as "dogmatic", "fanatic" and "fundamentalist". In this context religion is supplanted by a secular spirituality, or by something termed "spiritualities of life", which is a practice equating spirituality with the flow of life or life itself.[3]

## Christfulness, a definition

*Fullness* can be understood as saturation or completion. Connected to the word "Christ" the term *Christfulness* can be described as being filled or saturated by Christ, surrounded by and drenched in Him.

Christfulness can be understood as a continual progression which follows several phases; not just once in a lifetime, but throughout it, as a spiral process. For the sake of an overview you can describe Christfulness

- beginning as an experience of God's love in Christ as a protecting and accompanying presence ~~(Christ in me)~~ (christ with me)
- as an experience of "Christ in me, the hope of glory" (Christ in me)
- as helping you see Christ or the image of God in others (Christ in you), and
- as leading to a vision of a redeemed mankind as the body of Christ (Me/us in Christ).

As you can see, Christfulness has Jesus Christ as its focus point. This means that the presence of God in Jesus Christ is the pivotal experience. But at the same time the experience of Jesus Christ is as wholly and fully human – just as he himself uses the words Son of Man. Christ shows us the full realisation of human life.

## What does it mean to be human?

Christfulness can in this way help us to find answers to such questions as, "What does it mean to be human?", "Who am I?" and "What is the point of my life?"

When we look up at the stars, and see the countless galaxies and nebulae, when we see the infinite variety of life on our own planet, when nature overwhelms us, we may seek to ask, "What is a human being?" In the Bible the writer of the Psalms (Psalm 8) asks the same question, and relates it to the human's relationship to God and to creation:

> *"When I consider your heavens,*
> *the work of your fingers,*
> *the moon and the stars,*
> *which you have set in place,*
> *what is man that you are mindful of him,*
> *the son of man that you care for him?" (Ps 8, v 3-4,)*

Humans are like all life on earth. The human is created just like all other creatures on earth. We share the same elements. We too are living matter, we have a life or a soul like the animals; we have senses, feelings and thoughts. We too are spiritual beings; we have a part in an invisible, inner world – and are created as an open system, which can sense this spiritual world, and receive impulses from angels, spiritual beings and from God. But the human is also, due to God's grace, created in God's image with the purpose of growing in God's likeness. "Created in the image of God" means that the human knows God and can have fellowship with God, created for immortality. However, the human was in the beginning like a child with all possibilities open before him.

Through growing up the human was supposed to learn how to be a good steward of creation. God's image in the human meant growing up and taking responsibility for creation on behalf of God. This is why the human is asked to give names to the animals and is portrayed as a gardener (Gen. 2).

In order to grow into this task of being like God in serving love, the human had to know his limits – But this growing was cut short because the human refused to accept these limits and allowed desires for creation to take over (see Gen Ch. 3 v 6). In this fashion the human became embroiled in angst, envy, violence, domination at the cost of others – or the human became a victim of others' lusts, violence and power. This is why the natural order is unbalanced by our insatiable consumption and desires. The world around us and we ourselves are out of balance; We are not in harmony with ourselves, but feel like strangers in our lives and our world.

We humans are no longer ourselves. We live so to speak beside ourselves and not at the centre, in our hearts. We are not in touch with our inner child. We have lost that openness to the world, and no longer meet other people or existence as a whole with trust. Our relationships are harmed because our relationship to God is broken. We have forgotten that we are loved and cherished, and that God is always there for us, just as good parents are for their children.

When a Christian looks at the life of Christ, they see a person who lives out this forgotten reality. We see a person who has the strength to live fully in a serving love, and at the same time has a humanity that is fully open and soaked in God's presence. If we, therefore, wish to try to get back to the infant-like child of God's free and fully trusting relationship to God, and again be filled with God's ever present, ever attentive and affirming love, a love which brings with it confidence and strength to explore our world and apply ourselves to the tasks we find in it, then we must look to the Master, Jesus Christ. Christfulness lets us wake up to reality as experienced by the inner child of God, so we can begin to live from the centre of our being. The Apostle and Mystic St. Paul sees this as a gift given to us by Christ by the Holy Spirit: *"For you did not receive a spirit that makes you a slave to fear, but you received the Spirit of sonship. And by him we cry* "Abba, *Father"*. *The Spirit himself testifies with our spirit that we are God's children."* (Rom Ch. 8 v15-16).

This experience is what we in IML call a *healing of the heart*. We describe this practice in the second part of this book. Healing of the heart is a fundamental experience in all forms of Christfulness, and is the foundation of Christfulness as a practice of faith. The first aspect or phase of Christfulness as a spiritual process is about the love of God in Christ as a protective and accompanying presence (Christ with me) and either stems from or leads to the experience of being a child of God.

## Christ with me

Christ with me is, as we have seen, an experience of safety and certainty in being a child of God.

The love of God in Christ surrounds us on all sides. Jesus Christ spoke about God as his Father in order to say that we, in relation to God, can feel as safe as children with their parents. When Jesus is with us, this means safety and security in the midst of life's challenges and we can, with the Apostle Paul, experience that no power on earth can separate us from the love of God that is in Christ Jesus (Rom Ch. 8 v 38-39). Indeed we begin our lives as Christians with a promise from Jesus, that he will be with his friends at all times and in all places to the ends of the earth (Matt Ch. 28 v 20).

In the 23rd psalm David speaks of the Lord as his shepherd, and this experience of David's also applies to our relationship with Christ. This is why Jesus says that he is the good shepherd, who always looks after his sheep. Christ even gives his life so that his sheep can live and be protected from the wolves. Christ knows his sheep and they know him and his voice (John Ch. 10 v 11-16).

Every once in a while when I am meditating on God's Word and the stories in the Bible, I come to a place of peace, where I experience hearing the voice of Christ. Many Christians have had the same experience, and share what they have heard with others. The New Testament speaks about prophesy and different gifts of revelation; I often call it inspiration in order to avoid the misunderstanding that I am in some way a 100% pure channel for God, for, as Paul says, all such revelations must be tried and tested. When I meditated on the verses about Jesus as the good shepherd, I was given this inspiration:

*My friends! I have promised to be with you always and to the ends of the earth. No matter where you are, or what you experience, or your mental state, I am with you. You will often not be able to feel it, and feel that you have been left alone.*

*When two of my followers on Easter day had left Jerusalem and had lost all hope, all they could feel was doubt, dejection and despair. Even though they were on the way to Emmaus they felt as if the road went on forever and had no end. Then I joined them, but they did not recognise me. They assumed I was just a stranger. But through my questions and my words I opened their hearts, and when I – even though I was a guest – broke bread with them, then they recognised me.*

*In just the same way, I will often be with you, but you will not realise it is me. Perhaps you will meet me in a stranger who will ask you questions and talk with you – or help you.*

*When you are restless, full of doubt or without hope, when dark thoughts cloud your mind, or when you cannot find peace in yourself for all the noise and turmoil that surrounds you – at that moment, try to be still – even now – and breathe, deeply. With your breathing, let go of the turmoil, the pain, the thoughts, and let your lungs fill with fresh air – with the Spirit of God... You will become calm, and the calm, the rest and the quiet contain my presence.*

*Remember my cross, my pain, my cry from the cross, "My God, my God, why have you abandoned me?" You know that I was and I am near – even when life seems empty and godforsaken. There on the cross was God, in the godforsaken. The Word of Life, which became flesh in me, knew what it meant to feel that all was lost, but God was and is in me. From the cross I said "Forgive them. Today you will be with me in Paradise." From the cross through the words "It is done" I gave up my Spirit of life into Mary and John at the foot of the cross, and to you.*

*I am with you always to the very end of the age.*

It is not only Christians who can have an experience of *Christ with me*. In fact there are many people who have not grown up with the Christian faith, who in our time experience seeing Jesus in a vision or a dream. There are not least among Muslims many well documented testimonies to visions of Christ.[4]

The old Celtic prayer *St. Patrick's Breastplate*[5] expresses this wisdom and can be used in its shortened form as a sort of quick prayer or as meditation. Its great strength is

that it begins with creation: The sun, moon, fire, wind, earth and sea, and solid rock, followed by wisdom surrounding God's leading and protective presence. Then follows a clear focussing on Christ, *"Christ to shield me today: from poison, from burning, from drowning, from wounding, so that there may come to me an abundance of reward."* Christ's protective presence is called upon in all directions, and also in human relationships: *"Christ in the heart of every man who thinks of me, Christ in the mouth of everyone who speaks of me, Christ in every eye that sees me, Christ in every ear that hears me."* The prayer ends by affirming the faith in the Holy Trinity. The prayer can also be used in a shortened version to be recited (the Christfulness Mantra):
Christ before, Christ behind,
Christ to the right, Christ to the left,
Christ above, Christ below,
Christ around, Christ within!

Christfulness leads on from an external experience of Christ with me to an experience of Christ walking with us in our lives as an inner reality. Christ lives by faith in our hearts, for the inner child of God is Christ in us. We are formed in the image of God and this image is Christ.

## Christ in me

The Apostle and Mystic St. Paul speaks several times about an inner reality, which I call *Christfulness,* and calls it a secret, which is now revealed, *"Christ in you, the hope of glory!"* (Coll. Ch.1 v 27). *Christ in me* is about how each person is made in the image of God with the purpose of growing in His likeness.

In Hebrews, God's Son is described as "the radiance of God's Glory" and "the exact representation of God's being (Heb. Ch. 1 v3). These words express how God's Son enables us to sense God.. The Glory of God is the presence of God, which is compared with light which shines from an object. God as God truly is, is beyond what we can comprehend, but God chooses to be made known through the Son and the Spirit. When we sense this presence, we experience it as light. The book of Hebrews says that God created all things by the Son. Creation is God speaking, a message from God. This is why, in John's Gospel, God's Son is called "Logos", the Word, and it says that the Word was the light and life of humankind (Jn. Ch1 v.1-4). Hebrews adds that God still speaks, now by meeting us in Jesus Christ. John says that the Word became flesh, in other words as a person, and that we therefore see God's Glory in Jesus Christ. (Jn. Ch. 1 v14). God is in Christ.

When we say that humans are created in the image of God, it therefore means, that we are created in the image of Christ to be like Christ. To say "Christ in me" is the same as saying the image of God in me; it says that Christ grows in me, in the very centre of my being, and takes form in me. This can happen when my inner being reflects God in God's approach to me.

We are created to reflect the creative light of God, so God can recognize God self in us, and so our fellow beings can know God by the light which shines from us, as a reflection of God. This light is often not as clear as it could be; the mirror is dirty or covered over. But even when there isn't any light that gets through, due to the thick layer of grime on the glass, the mirror is still there, underneath.

What then can be the reason for this grime? It can come from our thoughts, our feelings or our memories. Our thoughts contain so many impressions of ourselves and others, of our lives, our successes and failures. They can contain ideas about ourselves, about God, and other people, but these are *our* thoughts, and not necessarily reality. Often they create a distance or separation in our relationships to others, to God, and to our true selves. We have made God, ourselves and others into objects, or things – something we can own, something to fear, something to win, something to lose. This includes our feelings, shaped by our memories. All this can mean that we live in the past, or in the future, but that here and now we are not open to the light of God's heart.

Only a new creation can break through this layer, for the more we fight it, the thicker the layer of grime becomes, and the further we fall from the centre of our being. In the beginning God said "Let there be light", and there was light (Gen. Ch. 1 v3). The Word who became flesh in Jesus Christ called the light into existence as the beginning of life. Christ called the human into existence by forming the dust of the earth, and laid his image in the human as a reflection of himself, the shining Glory of God and perfect image.

In the man Jesus Christ we see God (the Word, or Son, of God) and at the same time what a true human, created in the image of God, is. True humanity is a life lived in openness to God and God's approaches to us, and also a perfect reflection of God bringing life and freedom to other people. Jesus Christ embodies, then, in his humanity, God's original created purpose for mankind. In his human existence we get an idea of how a life fully soaked in God's presence looks, and see a life lived from the inside to the outside – that is, lived outward from God's image in the heart.

We need the Holy Spirit if this true humanity is to become ours. The Holy Spirit bears witness of Jesus Christ and allows us to see ourselves in the light of his life – to see the way we ought to be according to God's creation. The more we see Jesus, the clearer God's presence will shine in to the centre of our being. This is a searing light, which removes all the layers of grime, and cleans the mirror to be new. It's like the conception of a new life; Christ is born in our hearts.

From this point on, life becomes about living from the inside and out. Christ sits on the throne in our hearts and we begin to become like him from the inside and out. The more the light shines, the more the grime shows: Memories, feelings, thoughts and fantasies. The Holy Spirit drives us from time to time out in solitude, stillness and the desert, where we seem to be alone with the grime and the darkness, and where we must lay down our fantasies, thoughts, feelings and memories. But we are not alone. Christ is the hope of Glory. Our life is anchored in the kingdom of God, which is to come and which too is right here, right now.

St. Paul, the Mystic, describes it like this, "*...I no longer live, but Christ lives in me. The life I live in the body, I live by faith in the Son of God, who loved me and gave* *himself for me."* (Gal. Ch2 v20,). This is akin to Healing of the Heart. It can otherwise be experienced through prayer and guided meditation, which includes the washing away of false ideas in our minds about God, ourselves and the world around us.

## Jesus' conception in Mary and in us

The story of the angel Gabriel visiting Mary (Lk. Ch.1 v26-38) shows us of course a unique episode in the story of salvation. Nevertheless it can be seen as a model for Christ's spiritual conception in us. Mary shows us how we can be people who carry Christ in our hearts. This happens when we say Yes to God's calling and are willing to follow God's plan for our lives, which is the serving love as embodied in Jesus Christ's own life. Mary shows us the way to an ongoing life as Jesus' disciple. The Bible says several times, that she stored up the words said about Christ in her heart. Storing up words told about Christ, as well as the words that Christ himself uses, in our hearts, mulling them over and letting them take root is what we, in our lives, should seek to do as well.

The conception of Christ in Mary is interpreted in the New Testament as a fulfilling of the prophesy in Isaiah, which speaks about a sign from God, *"The virgin will be with child, and will give birth to a son, and will call him Immanuel" (Is. Ch. 7 v14)* which means "God with us". This is illustrated in the icon used by the Orthodox Church called Our Lady of the Sign. We see Mary in prayer, that is, with her arms stretched out defencelessly in prayer. She carries Christ below her heart in a

circle. Winged beings called Seraphim surround her and confirm that she is now the throne of God. At this everything and everyone must stand still and cry out, "*Holy, holy, holy is the Lord. Heaven and Earth are full of your Glory.*" When Jesus' disciples open themselves defencelessly in prayer, a similar miracle happens. Christ begins to take form in us. Our Lady of the Sign is related to one version of the Pentecost Icon. Here Mary can be seen praying in the centre of a ring of apostles, whilst tongues of fire from the Holy Spirit separate and rest on all of them. Prayer creates in us a space which the Holy Spirit can fill with the presence of Christ.

## The Jesus prayer, the classic Christ-in-me prayer

The classic expression of faith relating to Christ in me is the Orthodox Church's Jesus prayer, also known as the prayer of the heart: *Lord Jesus Christ, Son of God, have mercy on me, a sinner!*[6]

This prayer is rich in content, and encompasses two secrets: the secret of the Word or Name, and the secret of the heart. We have already discussed God's Son or Word, through whom God communicates God self in life for the world in creation, as spoken of in the first chapters of John's Gospel and the letter to the Hebrews.

The word reaches us in a special way in the name. God's name is I AM WHO I AM, which is abbreviated form becomes JHVH (Yahweh). This name expresses God's being as one, who is their own reason for existence and is not descended of any other than God self. But this name of God is hidden in another name, a human name, the name of Jesus. Jesus means "Yahweh saves". Just as God's name is contained in Jesus' name, so God is close to us in Jesus.

The second secret in the Jesus prayer is the heart, which is the centre of our being. The heart is the deepest level of a person, and in Christian spirituality synonymous with a person's spirit; in the heart, that part that connects us most with earth and that part that looks to Heaven meet with our relationships to others. It is in the heart that we can open up both to the spiritual world and to the world around us. We'll find our spiritual heart where our vertical and horizontal orientations cross.

When the heart is open toward God and is reflecting God's love in relation to humanity and creation, then our likeness to the image of God is intact. But when that contact is broken our heart is split in two.

When we meet God in Christ Jesus and are moved by God's love in him, our hearts begin to heal in relation to God, and we begin to find our true selves, who we really are. And then our relation to the surrounding world can be repaired. It is this healing of the heart that the Jesus prayer asks for, by calling on God through Jesus.

Often the Jesus prayer is linked with breathing, whilst our awareness is centred mentally on the heart. But the most important point is not which technique or physical position we use, but that we keep our focus on Jesus, reflect on him and to that end "say" his name. Alternatively we can, whilst inhaling, pray, "*(Lord)* Jesus

Christ, *(God's son)*", and whilst exhaling, "Have mercy on me *(a sinner)*". In this way the breathing can aid the meaning in the prayer.

The advantage of the Jesus prayer is its simplicity, which enables it to be prayed anywhere and in any situation, and in this way help the person praying to live out from Christ's presence in their heart.

## Christ in you

Through the experiences of Christ with me, felt as safety due to God's presence in our walk through life, we are led to the inner reality, which is that Christ lives by faith in our hearts, and that he is the image of God in us. At this stage the next phase in Christfulness lies open for us.

When Christ lives in us we wake up to the reality that every person is created in the image of God. This means that we begin to see other people and the rest of creation with new eyes. *Christfulness* leads to an active awareness of the world. We seek the image of God in others. This is why Jesus teaches us to love our enemies, and pray for those who persecute us.

Jesus Christ wants to teach us to abandon our misconceptions of other people as our enemies. He leads us to understand that we often make enemies for ourselves, or create the notion of our fellow humans as enemies. There will probably always be some, who behave despicably toward others, and there will always be people who behave as our enemy and think of us as their enemies, but Jesus does not wish us to look upon others as our enemies. Rather he wants us to see them as fellow humans, created to be children of God.

This is especially true when we meet people of another religion or with other spiritual views than ours. It also applies when we think we see other people, in our eyes, misusing parts of our religious practice and mixing it with what, in our opinion, are alien expressions of belief. Within IML we express this desire to see Christ in others as *the discipleship prayer*, which we pray daily, when possible at 5pm when many from the new spiritualties with a background in theosophy are praying for the healing of the world and of humanity, and especially for unity between people with good intentions:

*God, you who are I AM,*

*I see the work of your Spirit*
*in the longing in people's hearts for the peace of your kingdom*
*for the truth, beauty and goodness*

*I see the presence of your serving love*
*in people of good will and in all*
*who want to wander the path of discipleship.*

*May the power of your Spirit flow in us and lead us*
*to recognise all truth, and in practical service*
*May your Word made flesh, Jesus Christ, inspire us*
*to serving love as workers for the kingdom of God*

*May I find my place in your one work,*
*for the restoration of the Earth and the human race*
*– with a humble mind, in purity, truth, and love.*

## Mary visits Elisabeth

Just as the story of Gabriel's visit to Mary provides a model for "Christ in me", the story of Mary's visit to Elizabeth (Lk. Ch. 1 v39-45) performs a similar function for "Christ in you".

Whilst mediating on Mary's visit to Elizabeth I was given an inspiration from Christ, which sheds light on the subject of recognising Christ in each other. It also sheds light on the transforming power which lies within this recognition, both for peoples' relationships with each other and for all living earthly things. The inspiration was received at a time when the gospel was to be told to people who were, and are, under the influence of theosophy and the mysticism played out in the stories of the Holy Grail.

*I will teach you to see me in your fellow disciple, see my presence in creation and your fellow man. My disciples' fellowship is as brothers and sisters. Each of you carries me in your hearts. You will recognise each other by my presence in your hearts. And your fellowship and unity is deeper than any family bonds. Your fellowship transcends boundaries – national, cultural, linguistic, social, generational or gender. My disciples are one – together you are my body, you are like a cup filled with my loving presence; a cup which encompasses me and God-in-me for healing, health and restoration of the world. You are the cup of salvation, the cup of joy, the grail of resurrection life. For this reason I have made you into one body by my Spirit. Through my presence in the world in you, as my body you are the vessel of salvation for the world.*

*Yet the vision of my body as the Holy Grail, the cup of serving love, is not complete, neither for you, my disciples, nor for humanity as a whole or the rest of life on Earth. This I why I wish to teach you to see me in your fellow disciples. Each of you receives my presence in your hearts, and each of you feels in your own hearts the grail of my presence, the presence of serving love in the centre of your being. You are carriers of Christ and communicators of Christ. You have each been called to let people drink of God's love, poured out in your hearts.*

*See me in your fellow disciples! See them as a cup of salvation, a cup of thanksgiving, a cup of God's presence. See the heavenly grail in your brother's and your sister's hearts, and rejoice, for your brother and your sister have scooped up from the Water of Life and invite you to drink. I give living water, and I live in the heart of each and every disciple. See me in her, see me in him.*

*It is when you see me in each other that you understand, that what each of you are apart, you are together as well: The grail for the Earth, who lets creation drink from the love of God, my Spirit and my Presence, poured out in you.*

*I am the heart that beats, the pulse of life itself – the heart of the grail. I Am the One Who Gave Myself over to the darkness of death, to the womb of the earth, so that I could rise again and bring life to the world. I am the wheat seed, which is sowed in the ground to die and then spring up in life. I am the grape, which was crushed to become the wine of the vineyard. I am the one, whose blood was shed, and in my blood is washed away the dirt of a self-sufficient and ego-centred lie and from the idols in your life. I Am the contents of the grail, you are the grail! My blood was shed to give life to the world. You are the grail and the priests of the grail; You carry me to other people and to the creatures of the Earth. You lift me up heavenwards with all the pain, which comes with the un-redeemed earth and humanity – the pain that became mine on the cross, when I shed my blood for you. You lift me heavenwards in thanks and as a witness of redemption, for God-in-me and my self-surrendering love is your freedom, and the purpose of creation.*

*I Am in you. I Am in your brother and sister. Just as I Am in you, I will be for the whole world.*

*See me in each other, love each other, and be a song of praise, a song of joy, a song of freedom. A song of My Presence, a song of the voice of the Creator, a song of restoration. The song, which sounds out over the holy grail, the cup of God's presence in my disciples and in your brother-sisterhood – a cup held up for humanity and for the whole world. Let my presence and my serving love flow over from the heart of every disciple and every disciple fellowship, and from the whole body of Christ, and let it run down into the heart of the earth. Then will the earth sing, "My soul glorifies the Lord and my spirit rejoices in God my Saviour, for God has been mindful of his servant – humble before, now in glory."*

This inspiration points forward to the vision for Christfulness, that I and we are in Christ – that "Christ in you, the hope of glory" points forward towards a restored humanity and a healed and renewed Earth.

## I/we in Christ

*Christfulness* began as an experience of how Christ is in us, and results in a life in Christ. Just as God's word became human in Jesus Christ, then we in Christ are given access to the nature of God. God's image in us is made perfect in Godlikeness. Christfulness is stretched out between the sacraments, which comprise the ancient church's initiation ceremonies: Baptism/confirmation and communion. Baptism is about Christ in me; he begins his life in me and gives me the strength to serve. It's like dying to the old habits and patterns of life, and beginning a whole new life, i.e.

being born again. Paul speaks about dying and being buried with Christ in order to rise again with him to a whole new life (Romans Ch.6). But in baptism I am also clothed in Christ (Gal Ch.3 v.26) I become part of Christ as a branch is grafted on to a vine (Jn. Ch.15 v 1-8). Now a new life in Christ begins. Paul expands on this when he speaks of the congregation as the body of Christ and the individual Christians as parts of this body, each with their role and their gifts, which are used to the benefit of all. In Pauls writings there is a parallel between "For we were all baptised by one Spirit into one body" (1 Cor. Ch. 12 v13) and "Because there is one bread, we, who are many, are one body, for we all share in the one bread (1 Cor. Ch.10 v.17)

The vision for Christfulness is a renewed and redeemed humanity, which is the body of Christ. This reality is rooted in hope and comes to expression when we celebrate communion together and share bread with each other with the words of Jesus, "This is my body!"

Whilst meditating over the communion as an expression of the experience of "I/we in Christ" I received this inspiration:

> *The Master Jesus Christ says: When I broke bread and shared it with my disciples, I said, "This is my body!" This act of sharing the bread reveals the secret of the completion of creation and the redemption of humanity.*
>
> *You are called to be my body – each of you a working part of my body, and each of you vital for the welfare and the purpose of the whole body. You are in me. To-*

*gether, you are my body – a living, energetic, and Spirit-filled organism. Through you I still have body in the world.*

*Your fellowship reveals the magic, which maintains the world: that you share with one another, are there for one another, serve one another. This unity-creating magic, which connects heaven and earth, is serving love.*

*"My body, which is given for you!" From the very beginning of creation, every created being is there for the others and for the whole. In that way it mirrors my being, for I Am the Word, in whom God communicates to you. This serving love was entrusted to humanity in a unique way, for you were created in my image to resemble me. I entrusted the rest of creation to you, so it could find its place in the whole. You were as a mirror, which reflected love in attentive care and in the service of creation.*

*"My body, which is given for you!" These words have taken on a resonance, which encompass pain, for these were the words I spoke with the words, that the bread is my body, on the night I was betrayed. And again in the words about the wine in the cup of thanks, "This is my blood, shed for you!"*

*When your lives began to cease reflecting me in the world, the world began to fall apart. The magic of unity was replaced by the magic of power, of fear, of lust and self-complacency. This is why I appeared, vulnerable, with the magic of love and service in a world drenched in dark magic. I gave myself. Despite your vio-*

*lence I gave myself willingly and thus manifested my devotion and serving love as the stronger magic – a magic, which brings life to the dead!*

*I invite you in to fellowship with me and let you share in my love. Through this, the mirror of your inner self is cleaned, so my presence, as new, can shine out through you in the world. I call you, as new, to serving love, in which the world is new and whole. I create again devoted and serving love in you. When you share your lives with one another, a redeemed humanity is made and grows, which is my body, and which is a small foretaste of the coming completion.*

*I Am with you, I live in your hearts, so you can recognise me in each other, and together become one body.*

*"This is my body!"*

## Bibliography:


A Monk from the Eastern Church (Lev Gillet): The Jesus Prayer
A Monk of the Eastern Church (Lev Gillet) and Mark Melone: Jesus: A Dialogue With the Saviour
Henry Cafarel: Cinq soirées sur la prière intérieure.
Franz Jalics: Contemplative Retreat. An Introduction to the Contemplative Way of Life and in the Jesus Prayer
www.christfulness.net

**Introductory videos:**
Christfulness Meditation:
*Christ in Me: https://www.youtube.com/watch?v=gYlGDosmtnw*
Christfulness Meditation:
*Christ with me: https://www.youtube.com/watch?v=1L9VrUSx1Ok*
A Christfulness Meditation:
*https://www.youtube.com/watch?v=2kvY-sJri6Y*

**Related titles:**
John Morehead: Interview with the Danish Scholar Ole Skjerbæk Madsen.
*http://www.inthemasterslight.net/papers-and-essays/9-interview-with-danish-scholar-ole-skjerbaek-madsen.html*
Ole Skjerbæk Madsen: How to become a Church in the Spirituality of Life Milieus?
*http://www.inthemasterslight.net/attachments/article/18/How%20to%20Become%20a%20Church%20in%20the%20Spirituality%20of%20Life%20Milieus%20med%20billeder.pdf*

# Christfulness as a practice of faith

## A Christfulness meditation

Jesus Christ, send your Holy Spirit and lead me/us in meditation.

- Sit comfortably
- Feel the floor beneath your feet ...
- Keep this connection, but let your attention glide over to your breathing ...
- Concentrate now on your heart, and relax in your heart ...

- See/imagine Jesus Christ before you; feel his heart which is wholly open to you ...
- Relax in his presence. Breathe calmly. Relax in you breathing in the presence of Jesus Christ ...

- Let go through your breathing of everything that weighs you down, the old preconceptions of how you are, how others are, how God is ...
- When you breathe in, receive peace, joy, and love from the open heart of Jesus Christ ...
- With every breathing out your heart and your mind is cleaned more and more. And with every breath, Christ lives more and more in your heart and your mind ....

Music, for example Wagner: Isolde's Liebestod

- With the closing exhalations, send the peace and joy of Jesus Christ out to the world around you... (*the music continues*)
- May the peace of God, which surpasses all understanding, keep our hearts and our minds in Jesus Christ, our Lord.

## Meditations on the life of Jesus

During a meeting of In the Master's Light in Kolding, Denmark, our colleague Jørn Carl introduced this form of meditation, which is inspired by Sandomstiftelsen, Norway. *www.sandomstiftelsen.no*:

1 Sit comfortably and try to relax. Regular breathing is a useful way to find an attentive inner calm. Leave distracting thoughts alone. Repeat to yourself if you like, "Lord Jesus, thank you, that you bless." When you have reached as much inner peace as possible, go on to the next stage.
2 Ask the Holy Spirit to open your heart to Jesus and the Word, and to lead you in meditation and prayer.
3 Read the meditaton text (a passage about Jesus from the New Testament) slowly several times. Take note of the main characters and the story. Learn perhaps some of the words by heart.
4 Allow yourself to be drawn into the story, as if you were there. Listen to the voices, see the expressions on the faces and the reactions, feel the atmosphere. Let the scene take shape around you.
5 Give thanks, that it is the same Jesus then, as is with you now. Have a private conversation with him and the heavenly Father about the thoughts, the meditation has given you. What have you seen in Jesus? What have you seen in yourself? Which decisions should you make? Let the words flow freely from your heart to God's heart.
6 Seek an even deeper stillness. Worship Jesus; the one who is love, and who shields you on every side.

## Awareness Exercise:

If your body is tense it can prevent you from focussing and receiving. So it can be a good idea to begin with some relaxation. Suggestion:

*"Sit comfortably. Feel your body's contact with the floor and the chair back. Let your feet rest on the floor if possible – imagine they have roots, going deep into the ground. Relax your shoulders – your jaw – let your face relax – you don't need to think about anything right now. Sense your breathing – don't change it – just relax in it – feel Gods' presence. When you breathe out, release the tension and restlessness. Listen to the sounds around you – and just let them be."*

A help to letting thoughts go is to notice them – not to fight them – let them be. Your thoughts can be like small boats on the water – you are not in a boat, but on the bank, and you let them slip past. Or they can be like clouds in the sky.

## The Jesus prayer, or the Prayer of the Heart

*"Lord Jesus Christ, Son of God, have mercy on me!"*

The Jesus prayer can be linked to breathing, whilst your attention centres on the heart, but the most important thing is not a technique or a body posture, but simply to concentrate on Jesus, think on him and "say" or even better "hear" his name. Alternatively you can whilst breathing in pray, *"(Lord) Jesus Christ (, Son of God)"* and whilst breathing out, *"have mercy on me (,a sinner)."* In this way your breathing can support the words of the prayer.

The main strength of the Jesus prayer is its simplicity, which means it can be prayed anywhere and in all situations, letting the one praying to live out Christ's presence in their heart.

## Affirmation and prayer

1 *The Christfulness mantra:*
Christ before, Christ behind,
Christ to the right, Christ to the left,
Christ above, Christ below,
Christ around, Christ within!

2 *I am a child of God:*
I am a child of God.
I am loved,
and I have worth
God, I thank you!

3 *Peace:*
I rest in the room of peace in my heart
and find myself loved by God.
From my room of peace
I see my fellow humans and my fellow beings
without judgement and foster God's presence in them.

4 *I bring Christ to the world:*
In meeting God's love I open myself to the Holy Spirit,
so Christ can live in my heart and make his likeness in me.
I bring Christ to the world.

5 *Always in God's love:*
No power on earth
can separate me from the love of God
that is in Christ Jesus.
God, I thank you!

6 *Freed from illusions:*
By focussing on the light of Christ and the creating word of God
I rediscover my true self, created in God's image,
and break out of my captivity in my false conceptions,
created in the image of my desires.

7 *The light of the world:*
You, oh Christ are the light of the world!
I am a child of light
I am light in your light, oh Christ!

8 *United with God in Christ:*
I am the bride of Christ.
United with God in Christ
I manifest the grace of God
by care for the world and in the knowledge
that a never ending stream of blessing and life
stand ready for creation.

9 *Strength:*
God's love and will
set me free in Christ
from all angst and every unhealthy desire,
let me find my true self,
and give me the strength
to pursue my calling in life.

*10 Created to be like God:*
I am created in God's image
to be like God.
This is how God has met me in Christ.
God, I thank you!

## Prayer for others

### *1 Healing of the Heart*

When *"In the Master's Light"* (IML) has a stand at various fairs for alternative beliefs, we offer the guests prayer for healing of the heart. IML also uses the Healing of the Heart in combination with pastoral care, and at Church services during times of praying with individual participants in the service. IML have monthly healing services.

Healing of the Heart involves reaching peace in the heart and healing in relationship to God, oneself and other people. You can experience healing of the heart through other's prayer for you, but we advocate that people also pray for themselves; Here follows an example of how to pray for healing of the heart:

Begin by praying:
*"Come Holy Spirit in the name of Jesus Christ. Show me how the love of God is flowing right now from God's heart through the heart of Jesus Christ and in to my own heart. Let me know in my own heart that I am loved by God, are precious in God's eyes, and are loved for who I am."*

See now how the love from God's heart is like a running river, a tranquil river, in which you can splash as a free and carefree child. See how you afterwards can lie on its banks and relax in the green grass. Fill yourself in the knowledge that you are God's beloved and free child, and that you have your well-being in God's peace and presence.

It may be that the Holy Spirit in the course of this process makes you aware of some obstacles and blockages in your relationships with others, to God, or to whom you are yourself. Try to articulate these blockages, and ask God to help you in eradicating them. Don't look for blockages, but if you feel something, you feel is too threatening, then seek help in someone else, for instance in a Church offering healing, pastoral care or private counselling.

End the prayer by making the sign of the cross on your forehead and your chest, using the words, *"May the peace of God, which surpasses all understanding keep my heart and my mind in the love of Christ Jesus."*

**2 *Christfulness prayer/blessing:***
When we pray with people about Christfulness, we follow the pattern of the Christfulness meditation.

Introduce yourself and if appropriate ask the guest's name.

Ask what the guest would like, and if the guest wishes a Christfulness prayer/ blessing, explain briefly, what Christfulness is:

*Christfulness involves being filled by Christ, and God's love in Christ. This is the secret, which makes humans whole: Christ in us, the hope of glory!*

*This means, that when we feel ourselves surrounded by God's love in Jesus Christ, and soaked in this love, we experience being completely us, as Gods beloved children, and God's light shines clearly in us and from us out into the world.*

Explain that this light, God's holiness or image in us, can be dimmed by worry, pain, suffering and false conceptions, which must be washed away, so the fullness of Christ can grow in us.

*When we speak of the hope of glory, it means that glory (God's presence, love and restorative light in Christ) is not something distant, but a goal, which affects our present time.*

Ask the Holy Spirit to reveal Jesus to the guest and to show Jesus' open heart. Pray for comfort and trust in God's love in Jesus Christ.

Ask the Spirit to help the guest to let go of anything, which masks God's love or glory in the person.

Pray that the guest will receive peace, joy and love from the open heart of Jesus Christ.

*With every breathing out your heart and your mind is cleaned more and more. And with every breathing in, Christ lives more and more in your heart and your mind....*

When you have prayed for a time and feel the guest has achieved this cleansing, you can say:

*With the finishing exhalations, send the peace and joy of Jesus Christ out to the world around you...*

You say a blessing over the guest.

## City retreats

Areopagos and In the Master's Light have for a decade organised retreats in Copenhagen in association with local churches, mainly as single day retreats. These go under the banner of "Attentive awareness in the city." We want experiences from other retreats to become a quality of the everyday life of the city.

City retreats are "quiet days" in the city, where we practice attentive awareness though our spiritual, mental and physical senses.

Stillness is a discipline, where we die to ourselves; our thoughts, feelings, ideas, opinions, speech, and where we withdraw from the noise of other's opinions, ideas, etc. Stillness opens us up to who we really are deep down: God's child, loved and valued, made in God's image.

When we gain access to this stillness, we encounter a new awareness – in relation to our surroundings, and not least to who God is, and who I am. Stillness creates, too, a new awareness in relation to the city, its inhabitants and its life.

A day of stillness in the city begins as we introduce each other and receive any practical information. Prayer from a Book of Hours (a breviary) shapes the day. We learn to pray when we are together at a service, in order that we can pray always, and in that way can subsequently carry prayer out into the city. First we pray Lauds (the morning prayer) with a short lesson on the theme of the retreat. After this we move in to stillness, and are led in to meditation through an hour's relaxation or liturgical dance. There is time for personal reflection. This is followed by Sext (mid-day prayers) with up to 30 minutes silent prayer. Lunch precedes an introduction to walking in the city, and then each person goes out into the city with stillness in their hearts and in attentive awareness. We can perhaps carry these questions in our heart: What pains God in the city? What pains the people there? What brings God and people joy and hope in the city? Upon returning there is a drink before a time of personal meditation, reading, pastoral care or confession. We meet again for Vespers (evening prayer) and the stillness is broken, so we can share our experiences with each other.

In Nicholas of Kues writings on wisdom (15th century) the learned Master meets an uneducated man at a market square in a town. The uneducated man demonstrates to the other, that wisdom is not the various opinions held in books; no, wisdom grows through natural observation, for wisdom according to the holy Book shouts on the streets, "Wisdom speaks everywhere, even here on the square. The world is God's book." The greatest wisdom can be found where you least expect it. It is easier to go on a pilgrimage or climb a mountain or go out into the countryside than to do the easiest thing of all: to see, what's right in front of me! (translated from Aksel Haaning, "Den kristne mystic – fra middelalderens verden", C.A. Reitels Forlag, Copenhagen. 2nd edition, 1999, pp 128).

# Notes

1 In the Master's Light (IML) was founded in Copenhagen in 1995, starting with "spiritual gatherings" and from 1997 engaging in Body Mind Spirit fairs and other alternative fairs all over Denmark and Norway. The aim of IML is to build bridges of understanding between Christians and people from Body Mind Spirit milieus, between Church and Holism, New Age, and Spiritualties of Life. IML is a part of the work of the mission society Areopagos. For the history of IML, see http://www.inthemasterslight.net/history.html

2 This summary of the world view of Mindfulness is based on articles in the Swedish Magazine NOD, Forum för Tro, Kultur och Samhälle, nr. 1, 2013, Örebro. The main presentation of Mindfulness is Jon Kabat-Zin's Full Catastrophe Living, 1990.

3 Cf. Christine Axt-Pascalar: Wie hast Du's mit der Religion? In: Martin Reppenhagen (Hg.): Kirche zwischen postmoderner Kultur und Evangelium. Pp 153-157. Ole Skjerbæk Madsen: how to become a Church in a the Spirituality of Life Milieu, http://www.inthemasterslight.net/papers-and-essays/18-how-to-become-a-church-in-the-spirituality-of-life-milieus.html

4 http://dgcoy.me/2012/04/03/muslims-experiencing-christ-through-dreams-and-visions/, see the videos on this page

5 The Full text of St. Patrick's breastplate:

I arise today
Through a mighty strength, the invocation of the Trinity,
Through belief in the Threeness,

Through confession of the Oneness
of the Creator of creation.

I arise today
Through the strength of Christ's birth with His baptism,
Through the strength of His crucifixion with His burial,
Through the strength of His resurrection with His ascension,
Through the strength of His descent for the judgment of doom.

I arise today
Through the strength of the love of cherubim,
In the obedience of angels,
In the service of archangels,
In the hope of resurrection to meet with reward,
In the prayers of patriarchs,
In the predictions of prophets,
In the preaching of apostles,
In the faith of confessors,
In the innocence of holy virgins,
In the deeds of righteous men.

I arise today, through
The strength of heaven,
The light of the sun,
The radiance of the moon,
The splendor of fire,

The speed of lightning,
The swiftness of wind,
The depth of the sea,
The stability of the earth,
The firmness of rock.

I arise today, through
God's strength to pilot me,
God's might to uphold me,
God's wisdom to guide me,
God's eye to look before me,
God's ear to hear me,
God's word to speak for me,
God's hand to guard me,
God's shield to protect me,
God's host to save me
From snares of devils,
From temptation of vices,
From everyone who shall wish me ill,
afar and near.
I summon today
All these powers between me and those evils,
Against every cruel and merciless power
that may oppose my body and soul,
Against incantations of false prophets,
Against black laws of pagandom,

Against false laws of heretics,
Against craft of idolatry,
Against spells of witches and smiths and wizards,
Against every knowledge that corrupts man's body and soul;
Christ to shield me today
Against poison, against burning,
Against drowning, against wounding,
So that there may come to me an abundance of reward.
Christ with me,
Christ before me,
Christ behind me,
Christ in me,
Christ beneath me,
Christ above me,
Christ on my right,
Christ on my left,
Christ when I lie down,
Christ when I sit down,
Christ when I arise,
Christ in the heart of every man who thinks of me,
Christ in the mouth of everyone who speaks of me,
Christ in every eye that sees me,
Christ in every ear that hears me.

I arise today
Through a mighty strength, the invocation of the Trinity,

Through belief in the Threeness,
Through confession of the Oneness
of the Creator of creation.

6 In my opinion the best book on the Jesus prayer is *A Monk from the Eastern Church (Lev Gillet): The Jesus Prayer*